Bloom and Guts

A debut poetry collection

written by
Scott McKenzie

illustrated by
Chunhui Li

Bloom and Guts: A debut poetry collection
by Scott McKenzie

Copyright © 2023 Scott McKenzie

ISBN: 9798398209617

Cover design and illustrations copyright © 2023 Chunhui Li

For mum, dad, Alistair, Fiona, and
my wife, The Amazing Amber.

Y'all are pretty gosh darn wonderful.

Abracadabba dabba doo!

CONTENTS

1	**I. Like a dream**
5	The Mother and The Traveller
6	Look at the Flowers
7	Your Secret Collage
9	Lost Contact
10	Up and left
13	**II. of a heart**
17	She's not
18	LOVE
19	Together: An Adventure
20	The Best Beach in the World
21	When I Call You Beautiful
22	My Favourite Colour
23	Fashion by "Force"
24	Selfish Boy
25	A Date with Acid Rain
26	Mud
27	The Bridge between Us
28	When Words Mean Nothing
29	I'm there
30	What You Do
31	Stone
33	Fire and Water
36	DROPS
39	The Journey Backwards
40	What Are You?
42	Returning

43 **III. ripped open**

47 Darling, we have guests

48 Crushing Strawberries

49 OF FEAR

51 Real Horror

53 CandleWaxSecrets

54 A Burning Wish

56 Paralyzing

57 5 Minutes

58 Picking Up The Goddamn Pieces

60 Makeover at Midnight

61 Carnage at Dawn

63 **IV. kissed with fire**

67 Murdering Assumptions

69 To Assume

70 The Fool's Hat

72 My Mission

75 Catch My Rage

76 It's Easy to Explode

77 Who Started the Fire?

78 Learning to be Water

79 My Greatest Project

80 A Strange Dance

81 An Open Mind

83 The Grey

84 The Path I walk

87   **V. and then…**
91   Fragile
93   Hit Me
94   Your Head Against A Wall
95   The Lie
97   A Little Reminder

99   **VI. planted in the earth**
103   Life is
106   A Reunion with Nothing

111   Cover illustration by Chunhui Li
113   Alternate illustration for IV. kissed with fire
115   Acknowledgements
116   About the Author

I.
Like a dream

The Mother and The Traveller

A mother met a traveller alone.
The mother was kind, she gave him so much,
but in time he gave up the love they'd grown
and soon began taking all he could touch.
When she could not sate the traveller's greed,
he attacked, hitting again and again.
Whilst ignoring other creatures in need,
he kicked her down. She bled on the ground then
she rose and looked through disappointed eyes,
shining far brighter than ever before.
You see, it is the traveller who dies
in shock… in his blood, all for wanting more.
So who was this goddess that knew her worth?
Never forget, her name is Mother Earth.

Written 2018

Look at the Flowers

Look at the flowers,
they are so beautiful.

Long ago I dreamt of an oasis,
a wondrous place of peace and acceptance.
Bright green meadows covered open valleys.
Trees stood tall without thoughts of dominion.
A raging stream was now a tranquil lake
echoing a sky without storm or cloud.
The grass was soft beneath my weary back.
I wanted to live there forever, but
everything seemed far too still, too silent.
Nothing died. Nothing grew and nothing changed.

Look at the flowers,
they are made of plastic.

Written 2018

Your Secret Collage

Close your eyes. Let loose any last random
thoughts. Night has fallen once more and now your
canvas awaits. Time to rest. Like always,
in sweet hope, you go where identity
is explored through collage that's real but isn't.
Stillness is what sparks this most private art.

So many materials here, for art
which makes no sense. But it doesn't seem random
when you're making the collage. Well it isn't
worth millions, yet this thrill-ride is like your
adventure movie. Each identity
is directed by one viewer, always.

Instead of just watching, you can always
be the star. Then see how alive this art
really feels. Find a new identity
in this patchwork of faces, a random
cleanup that's beyond conscious control. Your
collage is familiar and no, it isn't.

Sometimes an emotional collage isn't
pleasant. With the right trigger it always
has the crushing potential to scald your
soft cheeks. Problems pieced together as art.
How could this be practice? It's so random
that you prey on your own identity.

Wait. If you can keep your identity
then cut, paste, control this collage. That isn't
easy. It's rare to cut loose from random
weirdness and design playtime that's always
desirable. But it's possible. Art
with awareness makes wonder truly yours.

Open those eyes. It's time to pack up your
canvas. Day rises. Your identity
returns in one piece from the land of art
and secrets. This morning a collage isn't
within another and yes, as always,
what you do remember will seem random.

Your collage can be a haven, but isn't
home. Identity will no doubt always
make art. It's up to you what is random.

Written 2017

Lost Contact

I've lost contact...
with the me who explores
universes born from old terrain,
With the me who hides
among stolen tides
deep within my brain.

I've lost contact...
With the twisted worlds
which practice desire and pain,
reflecting days, so bold yet wistful,
unearthing whimsy fistful by fistful,
electrifying the mundane.

I've lost contact...
With the impassioned lives.
They are buried in the hustle of day,
sometimes bleeding through
like déjà vu
from what I see and say.

I've lost contact...
with the night
yet don't lament entirely, no way.
Shadows can be a thrilling meal
but I've a hunger for the real
and true adventures shine in day.

Written 2019

Up and left

They've caught me, but they're moving up and leaving me behind.
I'm caught between a hole and a half.
A hole of ignorance,
Half of myself.
I struggle because I am caught up,
So there is nothing left and it's hard to be whole.
Since I struggle to be whole,
Half of me fell into the hole of ignorance.
When I'm whole I can be caught up in the ignorance of myself,
Although, sadly I have nothing left for the pathetic people.
Good.
They wanted to twist me,
Fortunately they have just given up and left.

It's like I said. Say you like it.
They've caught me, but they're moving up and leaving me behind.
I am left to toil in a school of lies.
I'm caught between a hole and a half.
It feels like this. Loud and scratching,
The smell of blistered fingers and broken nails,
Scraping. Scratching up and scraping down,
A blackboard.
A hole of ignorance,
Half of myself.
I am running left field. Am I twisting up?
I struggle because I am caught up,
So there is nothing left and it's hard to be whole.
I dig ditches and crave to be whole,
While you cry over stitches and sing of the soul.
Half of me fell into the hole of ignorance.
When I'm whole I can be caught up in the ignorance of myself,
Although, sadly I have nothing left for the pathetic people.
This is telling isn't it?
I know, I am, telling on them.
Good.
They wanted to twist me,
Fortunately they have just given
Up and left.

Written 2012

II.
of a heart

She's not

She's not wanting you or thinking of you,
But that's nothing new.
She's not alone, so she doesn't need you,
And there's nothing you can do.
She's not the person you thought she was,
And you better back off because
You're not the right person for her.

You should run away and never look back.
Find brains off the beaten track.
Go away and no, she won't change her mind,
The good in you is too hard to find.
If you think there's something, it's nothing and she's not there,
So you better beware.

She's not an angel; she's a demon in disguise,
She'll break your heart before your eyes.
Here's something you need to realise:
Nothing is perfect and some loves are lies.
You are not you and she's not really she,
Because she's different now and you are actually me.

Written 2011 with edits from 2023

LOVE

Love is so many things
but to me it's a vine.
It grows across a lifetime,
overcomes obstacles,
and especially when
we're shaking at the edge,
Sometimes it's all we need
to live.

Written 2018

Together: An Adventure

Hey. It feels like floating to know,
Although there's always room to grow
we love each other's core.
So when a storm does roar,
the crashing waves won't scare at all.
Look! Are those vines ashore?

Thanks. My garden does need a wall.
No, I won't be ashamed
of the flowers that boldly bloom.
But yes, they do need tamed.
Else visitors will find a doom
of thorns, wild and enflamed.
Your sweet advice is also smart.

Yes. This mountain we made is high
and will not break apart.
These rocks I place that touch the sky
are here to lift your heart.
Alone, adventure makes me cry,
Together is what's right.
What a life! What a sight!

Written 2016

The Best Beach in the World

The waves were quiet that day
at the best beach in the world
No seagulls squawked or flew
The sun was shining that day
at the best beach in the world
Light hit the dazzling blue
The sand was so soft that day
at the best beach in the world
Where one path came from two
It was amazing that day
at the best beach in the world
The beach where I met you.

Written 2017 with edits from 2023

When I Call You Beautiful

When I call you beautiful
It means more each time.
When I called you beautiful
It used to be just your face.
When I call you beautiful
It's now way beyond the physical.

It's what you say. It's what you do.
It's who you are through and through.
Stunning on the inside and the out,
You're a sweet oasis in a drought.
Thoughtful, caring, and kind,
You're always on my mind.

When I call you beautiful
I hope it doesn't get old.
When I called you beautiful
I used to be looking at your body.
When I call you beautiful
I now look at you completely.

It's in your smile. It's in your eyes.
It's in your hellos and in your badbyes,
Your scent, your sound. You're smart,
You like it, you make it, you are it: art.
This is just one tribute, to not only your beauty,
But your brilliance. To stand by you is my pleasure and duty.

Written 2015

My Favourite Colour

What's your favourite colour?
For years mine has been found
flowing through fields turned ragged by waves
gliding across hills in a darker shade
and jostling all over the limbs of trees.
But now it has been shown to me
in a new light,
wearing a fleeting golden glow
welcoming the day or waving farewell
with a warmth felt by the still ones.
If I catch the dawn
or kiss the face of dusk
as it embraces trees, hills, and fields,
I'll find my favourite colour again
along with thoughts of her.

Written 2020

Fashion by "Force"

She takes my hand, leading me through
an uncanny land. A jungle so dense.
I don't really understand or make sense
of this project. But she knows what to do.
Still, I object to this odd charade
since I detect… vanity with my nose
as we walk through rows upon rows
of stock, endless clothes in a parade.
But I'm in shock as I look and smile
at maroon shoes, broguing, white soles beneath.
She helps me choose a watch with Roman teeth.
Brown, gold hues. Balancing sense with some style.

Written 2019

Selfish Boy

Look at you, in your big boy boots
trying to be a man!
How could you walk so tall
with a head so huge?
Leave being grown up to the adults, brat.

Look at your heart
pretending to be humble!
Gentle middle child, not so
amenable now, are you?
Sweet manipulation for number 1: horrid.

Look at your brain
pretending to be bright!
Will you ever think
about what other people feel?
A cut-throat race of invisible crimes: terrible.

Look with your eyes!
This low will go when you learn
and reach high, or you won't deserve a hug,
or a word. Selfish boy,
what you deserve is silence.

Written 2016

A Date with Acid Rain

Is that the time? Excuse me. I must go.
I have a date with acid rain.
Nothing left. Nothing to lose. Now I hope
she might melt away all the pain.

Sorry. Oh, pardon me! I need to leave.
I have a date with acid rain.
Maybe she will finally succeed in
fixing my foolish, frantic brain.

Out of the way!! I just cannot be late!
I have a date with acid rain.
We will stroll together with such passion
till no pieces of me remain.

Get your useless hands off me right away!!!
I have a date with acid rain!
This is all I can do. Yes, this is it,
the only love that keeps me sane.

Written 2018

Mud

Face slowly slips down
dragging head lower
with shoulders sliding further
as back sinks to ground
and feet shuffle sluggishly
getting harder
and harder
to move

Finally slumping
into a chair
dripping apart

over front
and sides

as outside

matches up

Written 2019

The Bridge between Us

The bridge has fallen down once more,
It happened almost like before.
Pieces plummeted to the sea
as we cried and yelled hopelessly.

A misunderstanding… again,
so getting across is doubtful.
We may build this bridge weak or strong,
still it's not *if* it falls, but *when*.

We forget the love it has grown
then blame it for battles we've fought.
We can, we must rebuild from stone,
Since it's the only bridge we've got.

Written 2017

When Words Mean Nothing

I learn and learn and learn and learn and learn I
but feeling, of blossom a only not am
a if all After habit. of blossom a
can? who word, their as good as be can't poet
die will lips my by planted promises so
clear It's hands. my by nurtured not are they when
creed: simple a need forever will life my
them of All deeds. are flowers but seeds are words
mean. to grown are they as much as only mean
forget. with frozen when blooms nothing nothing,
promises No earth. this on here right stand I
gardener thoughtful a before now wither
feel shall I wield. to rainfall and sunshine with
shame no more no more no more no more no shame

Written 2019

I'm there

Cover your ears and hear me,
I'm there to make you laugh.
Close your eyes and see me,
I'm there to love your smile.
Hug your pillow and touch me,
I'm there to hold you tight.
Hide your mouth and taste me,
I'm there to kiss your lips.
Whenever your heart feels heavy,
If ever your thoughts are too many,
and
even without being beside you,
I'm there
no matter what.

Written 2017

What You Do

It's not the glorious gifts you bestow
Not even cake in a box with a bow,

It's not your words showering me with praise
Though flattery butters up my heart for days,

It's not your smile, backward as this may seem
If found only in a smothering dream,

I don't know how love works, just how I feel
And fickle, fleeting gestures aren't real.

It's what you do
that shows your love is here to stay.

The way you sit and lend an ear
When I am lost, bent double by fear,

It's the way you take this clumsy hand
Helping me grow and understand,

It's the way you laugh, a sound so sweet
I know home is here beneath my feet,

It's the bond between us that never breaks
No matter how hard the ground quakes

And to prove my love will always be true
Through my actions, I shall cherish you.

Written 2020

Stone

This money-made world of peculiarities
formalities technicalities necessities
has wisened you
but also hardened you.
Like a stone you are stubborn
Sometimes sharp, immovable
Sometimes I think I'm your ocean,
changing you, showing you magic
as you show me different magic
along with how to survive.
But often I'm kidding myself
to think I am the ocean
since I'm just as rigid and brittle as ice
even melting under pressure ...sometimes.

Though when you feel the cool tickle of the tide touch your toes
you'll know it IS me
come to embrace you again.
Always returning (Never really leaving)
to wash away worries
despite stormy seas
which are part of me
but getting few and far between.
I am the ocean coming to touch your heart.

Your heart, oh your heart can never be stone.
It's the most precious amber in this universe
with a lily perfectly preserved inside.
Magic that's invincible
Beauty that's unstoppable.

Still, you are stone
upon which I rely.
Strong, so strong of mind, self-assured.
I can depend on you
and though we clash
through inflexibility in strife,
YOU can depend on ME
in this peculiar world
that's made from more than money.

Written 2019

Fire and Water

His is the fire

which glows softly,
warming weary bones
and charming hearts
with its naked kindness,
its sincere sweetness
in trying to be good.

You see, fire is simple: light,
heat, energy thriving in day.

Hers is the water

which touches gently,
soothing tense skin
and opening minds
with its wise persistence,
its flexible fortitude
in a world beyond darkness.

You see, fire fights the dark
whilst water endures: day or night.

And what if fire roars
with wrath that burns your hand?
And what if water erodes
the cliff on which you stand?
When safety becomes danger
and wisdom becomes stupidity.

Would you sleep beside the fire?
Would you keep your trust in water?

When water drowns the mind
and fire chars the heart,
memories still remain
of sun dancing across ocean.
From sunrise to sunset,
beauty abides in their union.

Would you cast this keen union aside?
Would you heed whispers of doubt and pride?

Wait. A question comes first.
Look inside the world's claws
and see. Is beauty still alive?
They may overcome flaws
if a heartbeat holds them together.
A hardy tenderness, a cause.

Will it survive? It all depends
on them. The world is chaos till the end.

Wait and see. You'll see
these two are always learning.
They know love is a promise,
not merely ardent yearning.
They talk and grow and dance
with her still flowing, him still burning.

It will survive through the dark.
Their beauty blooms, night and day.

Written 2021

DROPS

         Long ago in the night
      I   walked   out
   to follow a   distant rumbling
 Roaring   like   a tiger
              trapped
Then   the rumbling   stopped

All my hair   slowly
          stood on end
       and lightning
        leapt
      escaped
    screamed
    silently
    from
    my mouth
    towards
      the
    open
  waiting
    sky

    .

   .

  .

Then

my

nose

felt

a gentle

tentative

splash

followed   by

another
on   my   chin
My   forehead
My   eyelid
Sliding down
down
my
cheeks
Another   Another   Another
Another   Another

An   infinite   embrace   from   drops
of   water   without   judgement
or   any   kind   of   thought
Cool   enough   to   calm
Warm   enough   to   love
It   cleansed   my   heavy   skin
Making   me   light   again
Dropping   all   the   murdered time
the   numbers   and   words
from   my   stretched blotchy burning flesh
Then   my   knees dropped

          to   a   bed   of   lush   grass
blooming   with   bright   flowers
          They lit up the night
Turning   midnight   to   twilight
          Turning   me   around
Ready   to stand   up from the ground

Written 2019

The Journey Backwards

So then I said, "Enough!" and took a stand
by drawing a line in the sand,
but 'twas between left foot and right
away it turned a sorry sight.
Losing ground. Clutching straws. Trying to win
what? I argued with my ears in the bin.
"I just want you to understand," I said,
with blinkers on, stuck inside my own head.
But then I stopped. Started recollecting
the destination intended.
Pausing, listening, reflecting
showed me how it could be mended.
My judgement had gone astray all along,
so then I said, "I'm sorry. I was wrong."

Written 2022

What Are You?

Afternoon sunshine
tumbling down with petals.
A tear or maybe a few
running down my cheek.
A little bird
calling out through trees.
All the laughter
living in our home.

The frost on grass
when winter starts to squeeze.
The cold silence
when your heart slips from my hands.
The snowdrops raising heads
when spring begins its thaw.
The smile that raises spirits
when I can warm your heart once more.

The journey is long
and it is so very short.
With you I learn
With you I grow
I'm foolish and you're there
I'm brilliant and you're there,
shining bright, brilliant, and beautiful.

After years, it's easy for others to think
you are the easy option, the habit,
something that happened to me
which I never really chose,
But my love for you is not passive,
I do not take your beauty for granted,
your sweetness, your intelligence,
or the moments you bring,
both big and small.

I choose you every day.
I experience you
with open eyes and eager heart.
So what are you?
More than a friend, true love, or goddess,
You are life,
the bitter and the sweetness.
There is no existence without you.

Started in 2022 and completed in 2023

Returning

When sunshine spills to my neck from the sky
To the trees, a rustling breeze is a kiss
And with fierce tenderness clasped hand in hand
This ear is tickled by the breath of you,
I am bliss-bound, our necks entwined again.

Written 2020

III.
ripped open

Darling, we have guests

I drifted softly as a bird
That lands to rest near whisp'ring reeds,
When suddenly I saw a herd,
A mass, of squirming centipedes;
Inside a calf, their sluggish host,
Which lay right by a crooked post.

Its eyes were open, milky, still,
And staring at the cloudless sky.
They stretched the gash so wide until
Some blood had spilt upon a thigh.
I knelt down close, in search of breath,
To find the calf unclaimed by death.

The left leg kicked and jerked right back
As if it danced. To watch this pass
Was just like sitting on a tack
Or noticing the leaking gas.
It made me wonder what's inside,
If my own flesh had things to hide.

On nights when darkness feels so full
Or days when sound is hard to find,
The questions come, the push and pull,
To fill each crevice of my mind;
And then my gut to truth concedes
And squirms just like the centipedes.

Written 2021

Crushing Strawberries

You hold their heart
or is it their head?
in a trembling hand.
You see their face,
hear their damn falsehoods,
and curl those fingers.
You turn to stone,
a creature, something
with fire in that scowl.
You start to crush
a fool that cowers
and slowly crumples.
You lick the blood
which isn't bitter.
It's sweet. Mmm not bad.
You smirk at this,
now satisfied, then
wash your hand of them.

Written 2018

OF FEAR

I begin to reassemble
my tired, old body.
A hand
A foot
An ear
I still hear…
tap tap tap tap
tap
No. Oh my god no.
They've come back to finish the job.

We speak of fear like it's coming to get us.
We don't speak of what it gets us to do
once caught, contaminated, consumed.
We are the finger puppet
and fear is the fingers.

Whispers and screams
are haphazard seams
subtly stitching something...
something lurking.
A bond like love but not like love.
An instinct. For survival.
Or a twisting, pulsating, smirking mirror
reminding us the worst monsters
suckled from the darkest parts of our hearts.
Secrets. Born from sickening potential of the human race
crawling back inside the corners of our eyes.

The door creaks open and I crawl into the corner.
As that familiar metallic taste erupts from my mouth,
I think to myself:
Why does this keep happening?

Written 2020

Real Horror

Real horror
makes you want to scorch both your eyes
since you just want to escape.
Real horror
makes you want to slice off your face
with a rusty razor
since you don't recognise it anymore.
Real horror
makes you want to rip out your heart
since it's already in a hundred shards.
Real horror
makes you want to take a hammer to your throat
since all sound has long been taken from you.
Real horror
makes you want to smash your hands
since they've been frozen numb for years.

Real horror is in human hands,
it's held in hopeless hearts,
it's home in hateful eyes,
it's heinous and
it's here.
You see it in the corner of your eye
and back of your mind,
You hear it as the cruellest whispers,
You smell it as a rot which never leaves,
You feel it as maggots writhing within,
You taste it as barbed wire and acid.

Not secret, but not dealt with.
Truth is devoured by it
like a lamb which almost escaped.
Real horror isn't found
in cheap scary movies.
It's found in real life.

Written 2018

C

Arooked

Nnd wood

Dext I forms

Larkness to sit **this**

Eike **plays** a cradling blackened

Wven the **with** slowly my table

Ahich softer neck **the shrinking head**

Xt were than **of** frail candle

S last made all **a** flame

Epoiling marks my quickly those **baby**

Cverything for **the skin in promises**

Rhoking Questions wax spot, feels sunlight

Eip my Memories to my reality

Tnvisioning off brain. **Doubts burn arm**

She a this I Unwelcome away
   tupid! wax **new skin** need but
       That's drips name I to
          my **drips** Drip am
         old too Drip
          name **slowly**
            Backwards

Written 2019

A Burning Wish

Whoosh
How many times have I blown out this candle?
Grabbed evil by the throat,
All the evil that makes my blood burn
and sends acid tears down my face,
All the cruelty branded on this world
and the pain that could have been avoided,
The willful evil
squirming like a maggot against a wall
within my hand.

A coiled steel fist, cool from patience
is my other hand.
But my eyes remain hot,
staring at evil, incredulous.
But even if laser vision feels possible,
my eyes can't kill by staring.
So my fist draws back
and takes aim
at the maggot, the evil, the rectification
within my reach.

I strike
like a cobra, no, a freight train, no, an atom bomb.
I strike again
and again and again
and AGAIN and AGAIN and AGAIN
and keep driving my fist into the face of all I hate
until there are no more splashes of blood,
until my fingers are broken,
until evil goes delightfully limp within my hand.
Relief is released from my lungs with a sigh. It's done.

Then it changes:
the maggot starts crawling out from my grasp.
This is how it goes:
evil becomes smoke and snakes away from the wall
then I see the candle again in the darkness,
still extinguished, but waiting… as if it knows.
A hand reaches out from the dark but I block it.
I hit away another, and another, then grab one.
But this hand is my own. Another hand lunges, making contact.
SNAP

Written 2019

Paralyzing

It's too late
to tell you not to do this.
Freezing up
Paralyzing
Building your own cage.
What is going through your head?
Flitting between resignation
and desperation
Expecting me to grab a hammer
and shatter your icy prison with a single swift blow.
This shall not be so.
And as more ice creeps around
I beg you to listen
before it freezes over your ears.
Even a million warm embraces from those who love you
cannot melt the cage of your creation

Written 2020

5 Minutes

It started with one piece of ice
about the size of a fingernail.
He saw it on the side of his head
when glancing in a mirror.
He told his family and friends
but they said they saw nothing,
told him to pull himself together.
He went to the doctor
but they saw nothing either,
told him to speak to someone else,
who told him to speak to someone else,
who told him to wait two weeks
then speak to someone else.
This continued for three months
and then he disappeared.
After four months he was found,
Lips blue, flesh grey, frozen solid,
and everyone said how much they tried
to help.
What more could they have done
besides looking at him longer than five minutes?

Written 2019

Picking Up The Goddamn Pieces

Damn you,
You Monster, Fool, Ghost,
Or all of the above.
It's as if 'responsibility' is an alien concept to you.
Is it because no one was 'responsible' for you?
And you haven't broken the cycle,
The disgusting, deplorable, destructive cycle
of pain passed along.
So you attack, permit, or disappear.
Damn you.

The pieces,
Pieces of Body, Mind, Heart,
Or all of the above,
Are left behind in the wake of destruction you caused.
After seeing the consequences, do you care about what you caused?
And the cycle spins again,
The explosions rain fire again
on the heads of anyone.
So pieces need picked up, healed up, or locked up.
The pieces.

The pieces
Cut, Infect, Burn,
Or kill any who walk along
And touch them, or even touch someone who touched them.
All this because you failed to care for them,
And they feel it, your child,
The pain passed to the inside of their face. Your child
of suffering inherited from above.
So a broken thing breaks more, who break more, who break
The pieces.

Damn you.
Bandages, Anti-biotics, Skin grafts,
On the face of a child below.
Same as what happened to your face but failed you.
So why? Did someone or everyone fail you?
And people hope to break the cycle,
The fallout of all your choices, the cycle
of picking up pieces anywhere.
So chances are handed out, dealt out, or thrown out.
Damn us.

Written 2019

Makeover at Midnight

Minutes to midnight
and I've got a juicy beat.
All the stars retreat
from me, sharp smile, goal in sight:
It's makeover time tonight.
A chill owns each street.

This getup needs red
and purple round eyes to dread.
Anyone can aid
by dyeing if they haven't fled.
Crunch. Snap! Hot scarlet is sprayed.
A fresh style is made.

Written 2016

Carnage at Dawn

Oh no.
Not again.
The beasts have been and gone
and ripped apart their foe.

Carcasses litter the street.
Thin, black flesh with guts torn loose.
They were curious, careless, ravenous,
but found nothing good to eat.

Carrot peel, yoghurt pots, and fondue
displayed like an artistic dumpster fire.
Hey! The bin bags were just sitting there.
What else would cats do?

Written 2020

IV.
kissed with fire

Murdering Assumptions

Do you like my castle?
Been building it most my life.
Sadly, the foundations are bullshit.

Well, not completely.
It's just
hard to tell what to keep and what to lose.

The entire structure is infested
with falsehoods,
false friends who trip me up.

So after losing too many teeth
and spitting too much blood,
I have a new hobby.

It keeps my castle stable and
and I hope it stops me
from becoming a piece of shit myself.

I set the false friends free.
At first it was unsettling
since each of them has my smirking face.

But but I think I'm getting better
at it. Helping them help me.
They're not friends not friends not

They are not me.
I am beyond them.
They will will not hold me back.

Sometimes they evade my eyes
and someone else points them out
somewhere

my hands wrap around a neck
and squeeze
till breath leaves and the lie fades.

I'm currently repeating the process
weekly, sometimes daily,
and plan to con-continue indefinitely.

I cannot build without adequate foundations.

Written 2021

To Assume

To assume is to make an ass of… you know,
Plenty are ignorant, yet they put on a good show.
It's natural to leap daily to conclusions of delight,
We enjoy being smart and oh so love being right.

U and me know it's a race, not a fight,
Quicker to love or possibly quicker to hate.
Will we take the time to inform ourselves? We might.
Actions and knowledge hopefully make our fate.

To assume is to make… understanding come too late,
Correct assumptions are rare but still they're gr-r-r-reat!
I assume you like my "poetry" and I reap what I sow,
Each to their own. I don't imagine having followers in tow.

Written 2015

The Fool's Hat

The fool's hat is not of paper,
nor card, silk, or felt.
It bears no decoration,
no 'D' for dunce, no colours or bells.
It is of lead
and with every foolish error,
the hat changes.
It weighs a little heavier.

Real danger comes when the hat leaves
and the fool thinks himself wise.
He treats assumption as insight,
forgetting to try.
He only sees his crown:
king of the mountain, indeed.
A lustrous lie of course
for the hat never left his head.

With each good choice,
the hat fades a little from sight.
The fool's ego waxes
each time it wanes in weight.
Thus, when next he blunders,
his ego completely bursts
for the weight upon his brow
has now returned in force.

Yet, the weight of error is naught
when the hat is kept in mind,
when the fool tries his best
and bears the hat with pride.
A wise man knows
we are all fools, it's true,
lest the hat crushes him
and the cycle begins anew.

Written 2022

My Mission

Two lovers live in my head.
She is smart and he is dumb,
my mission is them both.
Let's start
with him, a perceptive fool.
Yes,
his passion has grown powerful.
So
he soothes or explodes
over and over,
This lover *chained to mystery*.
He sometimes brings exquisite scenes,
even fun and adventure.
But keeps leading her to hell and back,
finding nightmares who also return.
What a stubborn style.
He's the one who sours
everything.
He's the one who sweetens it too.
Without him,
she's **unreachable**.

It's only me
who can complete this
difficult mission.
Let's go
to her, an oblivious genius.
Yes,
her logic has grown languid.
Yet
she finds truth shining
amid darkness,
This lover *hooked on mystery*.
She has so many ideas,
creating actions, bold or subtle.
But sometimes she's so busy
they end up doing nothing.
What a messy method.
She's the one who forgets
everything.
She's the one who recalls it too.
Without her,
he's **useless**.

These lovers are my blood, my bones.
Without them, I'm nothing.
You'll find them listening or falling
to destruction,
creeping up. Nice. And. Slow,
or striking like lightning!
Forever holding hands,
they can do **anything**:
Make
a discovery,
Dance
as if possessed,
Give
a warm hug,
or even
Save a life.
It's not impossible,
even day and night meet.
He is Feeling and she is Thinking.
I must reconcile them
at all costs.

Written 2016

Catch My Rage

I want to catch my rage
before it meets the world.
It is far too stupid
to be trusted out there.
My eyes close...
Pounding. Feet down the steps.
I know it has begun.
Tables hit the ceiling
and land with a dull crunch,
Then curtains are torn down
and shredded like paper.

I need to catch my rage
before it hurts again.
It is much too savage
to be in control now.
Slow deep breaths...
Thunder. Plates strike the walls.
I can tell what it craves.
No. Not gonna happen
and there's no chance it will,
Even though the floor shakes
and the TV explodes.

I run to catch my rage
before it leaves the house.
It is still too heartless
to be set free from here.
One, two, three...
Silence. Destruction stops.
I think I've broken through.
But then more words are heard
and my hand is shrugged off,
All of the locks are ripped away
and the front door slams shut.

Written 2017

It's Easy to Explode

It's easy to explode,
to blink
and incinerate your life.
It's easy to explode
like a bomb
destabilized by strife.
It's easy to explode,
to burn
anyone who is near.
It's easy to explode
in a blast
of repressed fear.
It's easy to explode,
to break
and unleash searing pain.
It's easy to explode
with a boom
of screams released from strain.
It's hard to cut the fuse,
to think
so you can live.

Written 2018

Who Started the Fire?

Here lies the blackened corpse of Scott,
who was burnt out from the inside
but just started by feeling hot.
For weeks it was easy to hide,
till his fists blistered due to pride.
Thin skin was scorched in the onslaught.

Here lies the blackened corpse of Scott,
who could have stopped his fierce demise
but instead fanned the furnace. Lots.
Then only hearing truth as lies,
he couldn't see. Flame burst from both eyes.
The screaming inferno was caught.

Here lies the blackened corpse of Scott,
whose bitter smoke meets with daybreak
but none will watch when that face rots.
What could have sparked it all awake?
A hurtful word? His own mistake?
He started the fire with his thoughts.

Written 2017

Learning to be Water

I glimpsed a jagged shape
trying. To fit the world within.
Confident corners stabbed. Curves
and cracks began. To show,
to threaten, a swarm, of collected. Expectations
eroding
possibilities. The self-crowned king of.
Pretending kept setting. Itself up to suffer
so sharpness, rigidity, would be its undoing.
The pattern shocked the shape
Even rippling all reflections
so cherished, strangled dearly by a king
grown too vain and blinkered
Dissolving dripped like lazy rain
Never done since subtle jagged edges
strike back, but cannot win
now it grows beyond an object
This earnest vessel flowing with the world

Written 2020

My Greatest Project

My greatest project
isn't something I actively work on
all the time,
but perhaps I'm still working on it
anyway.
It's a meal that takes forever to cook,
a tower that is constantly rebuilt,
a mosaic of collected knowledge,
a computer reprogrammed day and night,
a portrait of a burning match.
My greatest project
wasn't started by me.
I have my parents to thank for it.
I've been working on this project
since I was born.
And they've always been there
to help me.
Someday I think I'll start new projects
like my parents did. These will be
so wonderful and so powerful
they'll even help
with my original project,
a book that keeps being rewritten,
a symphony of sweet silliness,
a map of a shifting continent,
a sculpture made from blood,
a tree that grows in sunshine and storms.
My greatest project
will never be complete,
but will be filled with love
when it disappears.

Written 2018

A Strange Dance

No
wishes
are granted
during her dance.
Tears begin to fall,
Inside, hope fades away,
She keeps crushing spirits with
only bare feet and cold surprise.
Young and old alike can take no more.

Yet her sister brings back such laughter.
Oh yes, this old duet has joy.
She spreads sweet smiles. Each sister
is a teacher. There are
those who think one must
die. No, this dance
always is
without
end.

Written 2018

An Open Mind

I have, well I hope I do,
An open mind for most things new.
There's plenty from forever, for you and me.
I'd been peeking through windows in my head,
Doors are now open for experiences instead.
There's much to touch, hear, smell, and see.

No matter how still, the world moves at a rapid pace,
It's miles away, but always in front of my face.
Awe follows many an opportunity,
Though I can't help being carefully carefree.
We make our mistakes and make them again.
Could our favourite lessons be the ones hiding?
The ones that sink in when we're still deciding?
We smirk at stupidity and welcome it now and then.

Like many others, I shout, "Embrace life!" Why not?
It's not easy, but you get more than you sought.
There will be hands to help and arms to ache,
Legs to lead, feet to follow, and backs that might break.
It's important for me to contribute.
There'll be eyes to encourage and mouths to motivate,
Ears to expect and noses to navigate.
If my mind is closed then so is my route.

It's madness burning every bridge,
It just makes life an empty fridge.
If your mind is shut, you've been shut down and cut off,
Barricaded from a world of wonder and questions,
A world where people can learn and make suggestions.
Let's use our hearts and brains, let's walk away from the ignorance trough.

With new thoughts we move with change.
We think on paths we choose,
We discover our stories, not beaten if we lose.
There are hidden victories in range.
Let's not wait to find out,
We can come to life and pick what it's about.

Written 2013 with edits from 2023

The Grey

When I was a child,
the world was black and white.
Heroes were heroes.
Villains were villains.
Problems could be solved.
The world made sense
and I was satisfied.
Then I grew up.

The world grew larger before my eyes.
I could hear the screams.
I could smell the flames.
I couldn't understand…
the schemes, the games, the politics.
Black and white became muddled, mixed.
All I could see was grey
and I despised it.

It filled my head,
choking my brain
with confusion and fury.
But hatred helped no one.
I had to learn
to survive, navigate, negotiate, "cooperate" whilst
retaining and renewing righteousness.
Now I walk amongst the grey

and see through it.

Written 2019

The Path I Walk

I vow to walk the righteous path
as long as I shall live.
It may be hard to find
in this world filled with grey,
but I know it is worth it.
Not for glory or gain
in the form of material riches,
but for the joy
that blooms from goodness.

Of course I will make mistakes,
I will be weak and foolish.
What matters is that I learn
and keep correcting my course.
I will admit my faults
but not wallow in them.
I will grow and grow
like a tree towards the sun.
Yet I will not look down
on other people,
I will listen to them,
think of them,
help them as they help me,
help them
even if they do nothing for me.

As I walk the righteous path
I will remember to laugh
at myself and how silly it all is,
find a bit of fun, a bit of pleasure,
without getting too serious,
but without getting lost.
Laughter is a fuel I cannot be without,
as is love.
Love is the journey
as well as the destination.
Love will flow into me
and shine from my words and actions.

I do not walk this path
because I was told to
or because I fear any fires of punishment.
I walk it because I want to,
I love to,
I need to.
I need to
live as a good person
or I cannot live with myself.

I vow to walk the righteous path
as long as I shall live.
There is no doubt:
sometimes my back will bear great weight,
I will become weary,
Yet as I walk this winding path
my feet don't need to bleed,
for I don't just walk this path,
I create it.

Written 2018

V.
and then…

Fragile

Have you ever wanted to rip them apart?
Fingers inside their mouth
Pulling
Pulling their jaw open
Snapping their head asunder.
You are the hunter
spotting cracks in fragile things.

The world will tremble
before wrath unimagined
Unforgettable
Unstoppable
Unleashed
Not just a burning beast,
A Predator
with Every single thing your quarry.

Necks to break
                        Eyes to pluck
      Skin to peel
                        Bones to crunch
Buildings to fell
                        Nothing to feel
Faces to bludgeon
                        Blood to spill
         Souls to steal

Baring your fangs in a mirror
You spot cracks
                        around the mouth and the eyes.
It's not the mirror.
It's you.   You who is fragile
            with the slightest tear melting glass of your cheeks
and the world gouging
those   visible invisible cracks.
You think   A little more and I may shatter
Then you say   It doesn't matter.

Written 2020

Hit Me

Oh come now.
Haven't we done this dance long enough?
The doubt the worry the failure the frustration the pain the suffering
The money the time the responsibility
The nonsense
you love to pull.
But like a ghost you pull your punches.
You pass through, possess, and play.
Poltergeist called Life! instead of tormenting me with untouchable tricks,
HIT ME
Get some mass and kick my ass
Knock some sense into me
Beat the ever-loving shit out of me
Break my fucking nose
Smash my yellow teeth
Gouge my algae eyes
Snap off my trembling jaw
Twist my spine
till it's no longer mine.
It won't be a picnic
but at least I'll know
at least I'll feel
where the pain is
where it comes from
and why and how and what
has been done to me
and whether I deserve it.

Written 2019

Your Head Against A Wall

WORDS
DON'T
WORK.
You don't listen,
They don't listen.
Sounds are just hurled
and people break...
So a wall becomes your therapist.

SMASH. SMASH. SMASH...
Pain is a distraction
from boiling frustration.
SMASH. SMASH. SMASH...
The hot stench of metal
trickles into your eyes
and everything is red.
SMASH. SMASH. SMASH...
That forehead is now stained...
numb... and cracked...

Imagine if they could see your thoughts
when they see your brain.
If only it worked that way.
Laughter bursts from blue lips
as you fall backwards
into the selfish sleep.
No more misunderstandings
...for YOU at least.

Written 2017

The Lie

Pain is rising above your chin.
Arms and legs already caught
Bent
Broken
Nearly numb
and within, something begins to grow.

Desperation spreads spores
like a parasite that rips away hope,
darkening everything before you,
blotting out every speck of light,
any chance of a worthwhile future.
Unable to move, unable to think. No way forward, no way around.
About to drown. Trapped.

They're back.
By your side when you thought they'd never return.
Your raft, your oasis in a desert, your light in the darkest cave.
Whispering promises of peace
Answers to any problem
The solution

You cannot hear, you feel. And it all feels logical.
Of course! This is the only option and it makes perfect sense:
Feeling right, doing right by you and right by everyone else.
Removing the burden.
Yet, logic is not logic when your head is being crushed
by the heel of the world.
When your heart is turning
to lead inside its cold, useless box.
When you treat relief as truth.

Each whisper is part of a lie,
the most harmful lie to exist.

The end of suffering.
The only thing their "solution" ends is a gift,
torn from fingers with no second chance.
Then it unleashes a whole new wave of suffering
to drown the ones who loved you.
Yes. They exist.
It would hit them like a tsunami,
filling mouth, nostrils, ears, heart,
making mind blank. Stunned.
Each successive wave hits differently.
Some are barely felt.
Some are like drowning all over again.
All this, for believing the lie.

And the liar... they sound like milk and honey.
They feel like getting tucked in
with a warm blanket.
They don't look like a snake,
feel like thorns,
or sound like anything other than
your greatest friend.

You may start to trust the liar
since they promise what you crave.
They can make the bad things go away
and you're a child again,
thankful for a parent here to fix things,
to save you from the world
or save the world from you.

I urge you to wait.
Wait. Before heeding their words.
Wait. Before doing what
cannot
be undone.
Wait. And the cracks will show,
the "logic" will be faulty,
the future will have more than a few specks of light.

Why?
Why will things be better?
Why will things be different?
Why bother
when the chance seems so low?

This, I cannot answer for you.
All I know
is that you can recognise lies
and you will always matter.

Written 2021

A Little Reminder

When you've burnt me down
so my flesh is grey,
When you've drained me of blood
so my strength would stray,
When you've crushed my weary bones
day after day,
There's something you'll witness
that terrifies prey,
There's something ancient
that fights like thunder in the fray,
There's something inside
that lights my way,
There's lightning in my eyes,
the kind that never dies.

Written 2019

VI.

planted in the earth

Life is

Life is pain.
It's bleeding and weeping
till only emptiness remains,
It's being so broken,
so numb from all the shards
you've been stabbed with,
it feels permanent.

Life is pleasure.
It's smiling and laughing
till your cheeks and belly ache,
It's being so delighted,
so warm from head to toe,
it feels just like
you've swallowed the sun.

Life is stupid.
It's making a habit
of thoughtlessness
and getting a taste
for ignorance,
It's closing off from the world
and from yourself.

Life is smart.
It's seeing the lessons
in the days
and letting go
of thoughts at night,
It's finding when to flow
and when to take a stand.

Life is prison.
It's being so trapped
by influence, by... fate,
that you stare at the ground
and amongst the dusty rocks
the future
is chained to your feet.

Life is freedom.
It's being so empowered
by effort, by conviction,
that you look to the sky
and before the blazing sunrise
the future
is waiting in your hands.

Life is evil.
It's a two-headed snake
called Radical and Banal,
It's spitting cruelty
from a heart that keeps clutching
to fear
and hate.

Life is good.
It's a pair of flowers
named Mettā and Muditā,
It's spreading kindness
from a heart that's still glowing
with hope
and love.

Life is a bunch of dreams and nightmares.
Life is an ox of glass, an ant of steel.
Life is fortune and misfortune shaking hands.
Life is fire and water embracing.
Life is a lot of mixed messages.
Life is infinite shades of experience,
some darker, some lighter.

Life is struggle
but it's also worth the struggle,
Something incredible is rarely easy,
Miracles aren't miracles
because they are perfect,
a phoenix rises from ash
not gold.

Life is a spark,
without it…
the canvas is blank,
the song is silent,
the box is empty,
there is no beauty
for it has no meaning.

Life is a mess,
a beautiful mess.
I do hope you agree.

Started in 2017 and completed in 2018

<u>A Reunion with Nothing</u>

I'm going to die
someday, somewhere, somehow:

Perhaps I slip
away in my sleep
at the age of 85,
Maybe next week
a massive truck
stops me from being alive,
Or illness in a decade
tightly grabs hold
till my heartbeat takes a dive.

Of course I'm scared.
Death is a stranger forever,
Life? The most familiar friend,
And to be frank
I may never be prepared
for that final moment,
for the question of more.
Especially since it's a mistake
to think dying isn't shared.

Yes, that final moment
can last
and as it does connections show
in the form of thread
between who has ever loved
or even just come to know
me, a thread being pulled down
who shakes the web with pain
as some struggle to let go.

Even if the end is brief,
if I don't leave piece by piece,
if I don't have a tortured pulse,
and my breath isn't viciously pinched,
there's still an emptiness filled with grief
that's always left behind.
Yet, in this tapestry so beautiful
it could be
birth shows death is not merely a thief.

Was it scary before you were born?
Before the womb, your first ever dawn?
I ask myself once more
like reaching through fog so thick,
a whisper to the dark
of a long forgotten shore.
Death may not be so strange in this fog
since it leads to something,
the nothing I've met before.

Those waters and I were one,
I was nothing, nothing was me.
It's held as unbearably deep, monstrous,
But I reject the dreadening mistruth
of "nothingness" being opposite from the sun,
same as "darkness", same as "coldness".
Such things are cast off at closing
then an epilogue of ripples shall come,
same as the prologue before I'd begun.

Bewilderment
brings questions out.
Why would death be a lonely land?
Why would regret fill a raindrop?
Pain felt by atoms? A mix-up.
I'll be kin to stars, like grains of sand,
one with tapestry *and* water,
a wonder unaware
with nothing to fear or understand.

My remains shall meet the earth
and start collaborating slowly
with all things as they spin
disconnecting, reconnecting strands
nurturing a new kind of worth.
Countless pathways open, fervently
showing what seems final
is actually forever
when my final breath brings birth.

The soft sky has it,
a reminder there, everywhere, that
I must treasure this fortune whilst here.
It's natural to mourn,
yet, when my gift of time is gone
I give space to life when I disappear.
Amongst worms and moles and trees
so glorious, a truth lives
like a star beyond reach though still so clear:

A reunion with nothing
is a reunion with the universe.

Started in 2018 and completed in 2019

WITH THANKS TO:

Mum and dad for nurturing my adoration of stories and for their unconditional love and support. When my mental health was at its lowest, they helped me get back on track and grow into someone I'm happy being.

Thank you to Alistair and Fiona for reading my creations and for being hilarious, kind-hearted human beings who love stories as much as I do.

Thank you to Amber (Zixuan), my incredible wife who has stuck with me through highs and lows, always helping me to improve. And for reading everything I write, even through all the times I have said, "I'm going to write," without actually writing anything.

Thank you to Amanda Anderson for encouraging me and giving advice about publishing my poetry in collected form as she has done.

And a huge thank you to Chunhui Li for not only providing guidance on how to publish this collection, but for making this book more beautiful than I ever imagined it could be. Her artwork is gorgeous and I'm so incredibly lucky that she used her time and effort for this project.

And to everyone else who has supported my writing, either by reading it and giving feedback, or by giving me inspiration.

ABOUT THE AUTHOR

Scott McKenzie has been a human for years and he has said on record that it continues to be an incredible experience.

He fell in love with stories when he was a boy and since then has expressed his creativity in various ways. For a long time, he drew spaceships, robots, aliens, superheroes, and more; then it was poetry which took his attention (an excellent way to get straight to matters of the heart); and now he focuses on creating short fiction which aims to not only disturb and excite, but also to truly move the heart and mind.

Printed in Great Britain
by Amazon